Puppy Training

Learn How to Easily and Effectively Train Your Puppy

Zach Rucker

Want a Free E-Book?

Signup for the Gamma Mouse Media Newsletter and pick a free e-book as a Thank You Gift.

For more details and to sign-up, visit http://www.gammamouse.com.

Preparing to Train Your Puppy – Get the Facts before You Start

Puppies are the epitome of cuteness. Little wags of their tails and a whimper have their owners doting all over them! Sadly this isn't the best way to have a well-adjusted grown dog. In order to have a good adult dog training must start when it is still a puppy. Basic tricks are nice, yes but your dog should also walk well on a leash, have a recall (return when called) and be able to handle different situations well.

Potty Training.

Much like children you need to teach your puppy where and when it is acceptable to go to the bathroom. At the age of 12 weeks puppies have little no to control over when and where they go. In general puppies should follow the "hour to month" rule. If your puppy is four months old they'll be able to wait around 4 hours to go potty. At night, by four months, your puppy should be able to hold it overnight. Establish a regular feeding schedule alongside your puppy out time and potty breaks. When outside try to take your puppy to a certain spot to go to the bathroom, this helps it associate inside and outside. Don't forget to praise your puppy when it does go potty in the right spot!

No-Bite Training.

Many, if not all, puppies go through a stage of biting everything from your hand to your stocking feet. As soon as biting begins it should be nipped in the bud, so to speak. Your puppy doesn't really intend to hurt you when they bite, they explore much of the world with their mouths. When your puppy mouths you pay close attention. When the bite gets too hard or starts to hurt be sure to let out a loud sound. Yelps and "Ow" do well. The startle of volume will make him stop biting. When he releases walk away for a short period of time (10-20 seconds) then resume playing. It takes time but your puppy will catch on and learn that biting is something he or she shouldn't be doing.

Recall Training.

One of the most important 'tricks' your puppy can learn is to come when called. This simple trick can save you from hours of chasing a loose puppy or even save your puppies life should he take off and be in the line of danger. Start with your puppy on a leash. You want to move a few feet away with either your puppies' favorite treats or toy. Encourage your puppy by saying his name without applying any pressure to the leash. Pat your knees, make yourself be exciting and fun. As soon as your puppy starts towards you say 'come!' Once he gets to you praise and reward for the good behavior. Continue to do this from distances further away. By making the recall a game you'll find your puppy more eager to come when called. Once he or she has mastered this on the leash start trying it in the home or at the dog park while playing. Make sure you have your treats ready!

Training a puppy is hard work, you should always do your research before getting a puppy. Make sure everyone in the house is aware of what the puppy is and is not allowed to do. Finding a local professional trainer with good reviews is a good place to start if this is your first puppy. Having a professional there will help you best cope with your little fur ball and learn the steps to having a well behaved, calm dog who's always under control.

The Fundamentals of Puppy Training – What You Need to Know Before it is Too Late

Puppy training is a very important aspect in the growth and development of a dog. This is due to the fact that it plays a great role in determining the manner in which the puppy will behave once it is a fully grown dog. Many at times, puppy training is an activity that is left out to some of the professional pet instructors.

However, this is a job that can be carried out by any individual provided he or she is well versed with all the basic puppy training principles. With knowledge on these principles, an individual is in a position to know how to handle a puppy in the course of its training. Some of the most critical puppy training principles are discussed below.

Knowledge

The most basic puppy training principle is having the knowledge and know-how of all techniques and rules to observe prior to training a puppy. As a matter of fact, you must have a set of guidelines that will assist you to make some important decisions and evaluations before the dog training begins. For the training to be a success, it is important that all the knowledge is used and implemented so as to have a reflection of the training results.

Consistency

This is another important guideline among the numerous basic puppy training principles. When training your puppy, it is very difficult for it to master and comprehend an instruction with only a single command.

This therefore means that you should exercise a repetitive administration of commands so that they can stick in the puppy's mind. A very single command can be repeated should be repeated as many times as possible up to the moment a perfect and ideal result is achieved.

However, a single command should not be repeated for so long. It is important to have an interval between commands so that the puppy does not get bored and start offering some resistance.

Rewarding

This is a principle that may seem awkward but it is one that is very important. It is essential to show some appreciation to your puppy's efforts. This is an aspect that goes a long way in maintaining the puppy's enthusiasm and motivation to its training program. A reward for the puppy must not necessarily mean offering it a piece of meat or something to eat. A gentle pat on the back can do the trick. In addition, the trainer can slowly caress its fur and with that, the puppy will sense that it has done what it was supposed to.

Be patient

Unlike human beings, puppies may not have a very high IQ level and therefore it may take some time for them to master a particular command. It is therefore important that the trainer remains patient with the puppy. Do not rush the puppy to master many commands within a short time. The trainer must exercise a high level of self-control if all the commands are to be appropriately executed.

Putting It All Together

Puppy training is an activity that has an immense contribution to a dog's life in terms of behavior and response. It is therefore important to introduce your puppy to such training at a very young age, probably at the tenth week.

Stop Unnecessary Potty Accidents Before They Occur

Getting a new puppy is always exciting to many. What is much greater is having your puppy relieving itself outside the house hence maintaining a clean and fresh environment. Let's look at how to housebreak your puppy. Housebreaking is not entirely a hard task but it certainly requires patience and commitment to get that puppy keeping you happy. You might want to work with the following steps as you work to housebreak your puppy.

Get a routine

Establish a routine for your puppy by feeding him on schedule. Scheduled feeding helps much since dogs also tend to relieve themselves on schedule if the proper schedule is followed. A schedule will teach a dog that there is time for everything in its life, feeding, playing and eliminating waste. For every single month of age, a puppy can hold his bladder for approximately one hour. So as the months progress so do the number of hours the puppy will be able to hold its bladder. This should work to help you establish that routine.

Frequently take the puppy outside

Immediately after he wakes up, take your puppy outside. During plays and immediately after eating or drinking, you need to take him outside. As a puppy eats, the food exerts pressure on the colon and thus the need to defecate. This frequent display of the need to leave the house will show your puppy that whenever he feels to go potty, he should go outside.

Choose a spot for your puppy outside to go potty

Dogs require a familiar environment and smell to be comfortable to defecate. The associate the smell and place with their bathroom calls and due to the need to stay clean, dogs will use one spot to relieve themselves. Therefore, pick a spot for your puppy and always take him there until he is accustomed to that area.

Reward them for eliminating outside

Puppies learn things mostly through receiving treats for doing well in such. Every time your puppy finishes outside, give him a treat or praise him and he will know for sure that is what he is supposed to do.

Confinement

Let's say you won't be able to keep an eye on your puppy for a while and you don't want them soiling your house, you might want to confine him to a small space. The feeling of a small face will put off a puppy's need to defecate and will wait until it is set free. Just make sure he is comfortable.

Watch over your puppy

Supervise your puppy to ensure he follows what you have taught him. If you get him making a mistake, interrupt immediately and take him outside to his designated spot. Wait for him to finish and reward him for that. This will make him learn his mistake and change for good. Do not shout or punish the puppy as it might think its body mechanisms are wrong and may lead to a medical condition in a bid to please you.

Watch for signs of wanting to eliminate like barking or scratching the floor and take him outside.

When travelling

Choosing a good pet sitter will help keep your puppy in check and hence reduce the chances of him reverting back to soiling your house once you get him back.

Many think housebreaking is such a hard task. The joy is in the reward you get when you are through with all the training. Once established and done right, housebreaking your puppy could be the easiest job you will have to undertake.

Don't Jump On That – How to Break Your Puppy's Bad Habit

One of the best things of having a dog is that there will always be someone anxiously waiting for you at home, who greets you with joy when you arrive, this feeling sure is really amazing. However, a dog that constantly is jumping up can be really annoying. For that reason it is convenient to train your dog not to jump up since he is a puppy. How can you do that? Here are 5 easy tips that will make your dog stop jumping up. This doesn't mean your dog will stop receiving you joyfully, it just means that the annoying part is going to disappear.

1) Ignore your puppy

We know that ignoring a cute puppy is probably one of the most difficult things to do. However this is the most effective alternative to make the jump up stop. When your dog is jumping, remain in the same place without moving. Do not look or say anything. Wait patiently and reward him enthusiastically when he calms down (this is the right moment to say hello to your dog!). The puppy will eventually associate the reward with calming down, most of the times they do it quite fast.

2) Invade your puppy's space

One of the things that you probably do when your dog jumps at you, is throwing yourself back. If you do that, you are just giving your dog more space, and dogs perceive that as if you were inviting them to play. This might sound weird, but next time your puppy jumps up to you, bend down to be at his level, you won't even have to say anything. This method is pretty effective and works with most puppies.

3) Give your puppy "the signal"

This tricky tip consists on making a facial expression with your mouth open, you have to remain quiet but with pretty visible teeth. How does making this face works? It's simple, this is a signal that adult dogs use to calm their puppies, it works naturally (and it's actually really fun to do it!). If you want to use "the signal" it's really important that you make direct eye contact with your dog at the time, otherwise this method is not going to work.

4) Teach your puppy "the command"

Think of a word that can function as a single command, exclusively used to order your dog not to jump up. Use this work firmly every time your puppy does it. He will associate this particular word to stop jumping. In order to make the command work it is important to physically or verbally reward your puppy for following the command, this way your dog will always be sure that if he calm after hearing the command he is going to be rewarded.

5) Be consistent with your puppy

Finally, no matter which method you decide to use the key is to always be consistent. Patting the puppy one day when he is jumping, and getting angry with the day after is not going to help. You need to be consistent in order for your dog to understand that is not good to jump up.

Keep Your New Puppy from Destroying Your Precious Furniture

All dogs have a period in life where they chew and destroy objects around the house. This thing is normal to happen to puppies when they change their teeth. Change of teeth irritates the gums and if it's not watched closely, the puppies can destroy furniture in an attempt to eliminate this stress. But there is a good news: once the dentition is complete, most of the times the problem is solved. But there are puppies who keep chewing objects even after the change of teeth has happened.

Why adult dogs chew objects around the house?

The fact that the dog keeps chewing is a sign of stress. It can be caused by changes in the meal programs, diet, type of food or even the change of the schedule. Dogs might end up destroying the furniture if the master has no authority over the animal and it's not considered the leader of the pack. But keep in mind, dogs have short time memory and correction methods should be applied while performing the fault or immediately after the fact. Otherwise, the dog will not associate the correction with his conduct, but rather consider it unjustly. Chewing up objects and following behavior of the dog can be educated if the master encourages games using balls or other objects instead of the furniture.

How to teach your dog not to chew and destroy your furniture?

The first step in the training of adult dogs is to identify the stress that is being put on the animal. Then start working to achieve and maintain authority. For the first lesson of obedience, the dog has to learn easy commands like sit, down or walk. At first, the owner of the dog should work with the pet at least one hour a day on those commands in the house. After a while, the dog should be taken in foreign areas, for one day a week and train there. Don't forget to praise the dog and show enthusiasm every time the animal is having a good reaction on the commands.

Ignore the dog for a few minutes after you get home!

Praise and encouragement should not be given in the front door. So just after you get home, ignore the animal for a few minutes. Stress is linked to the owner's departures, and the door is where there dog is usually feeling frustrated. The rule is difficult to follow, because of all the excitement and enthusiasm the dog shows when you return home, but try and resist of the temptation of comfort in the doorstep. How to make sure your lessons were useful? When the animal is left alone in the house, don't forget to throw him a bone before you leave. That way you help the dog to release the stress of being without his master and in exchange he won't destroy any of your belongings. When you're at home and you see that your dog tries destroy the furniture, instead of shouting at him, try and distract him and throw him a bone. Don't forget to praise enthusiastic when the dog shows interest.

Thank You!

I hope you have found this beginner's guide to puppy training helpful and rewarding. I've always felt that knowing where to start on any new topic was the most difficult part. Hopefully this book has given you a starting point from which you can continue.

I wish you all the best in your puppy training endeavors!

Free Bonus Book

Thank you so much for your purchase. As an additional bonus we are including another great book, Ketogenic Diet by Nicole Harrington for you.

I hope you enjoy!

Ketogenic Diet
The Effective and Safe Way to Lose
Weight and Regain Your Life

Nicole Harrington

The Amazing Ketogenic Diet

The idea of ketogenic dieting is not peculiar. As a matter of facts, ketogenic diet has been there in many forms and in many variations. It has got many similarities to the Atkins diet. By the end of this article, you will be able to find what exactly ketogenic diet is, how and reasons why it works. Otherwise, it is good to note that, ketogenic exists in three different types: the Targeted ketogenic diet, cyclical ketogenic diet and the Standard Ketogenic diet. They are almost the same but differ according to limits and timing of carbohydrates consumption.

So, what is the Ketogenic diet?

In simple terms, ketogenic diet can be defined as any diet that forces the body in a process known as the Ketosis, whereby extra fats are burned as an alternative of carbohydrates which is used as energy. The right ketogenic diet requires the dieter to consume high amount of fat, sufficient amounts of protein and very small amounts of carbohydrates. It is also good to note that, bodies are of the character that, they turn extra carbohydrate in glucose which is sent to all over the body in energy form. When you enter ketosis by sufficiently restricting your carbohydrate consumption, your livers begin breaking down fat cells into fatty acids and ketones, which is supposed to be used as the energy.

How does ketogenic diet work?

Just like any other diet that you know of, ketogenic diet works by reducing the amount of calories you consume, in turn creates a caloric shortfall where the body burns more energy than it takes. That is the basic science of weight loss, and even though the argument is subjected to further debating, few shall be of the opinion that, all successful diets depends on caloric limitation, in one way or another. The following are some of the advantages of ketogenic diet:

It helps in controlling blood sugar and minimizing insulin spikes

When you consume carbohydrates, your blood sugar level would increase tremendously; this will also cause the fast insulin reaction from the pancreatic gland. This insulin is useful in dispersing excess blood glucose, which makes you to feel hungry almost immediately. And if you eat a low carbohydrate diet, you succeed in keeping your blood sugar levels low and hence the carb that induces hunger spikes are avoided. Reducing hormone level is the top priority for any diet so does ketogenic diet. Insulin should be reduced because it is the hormone that induces the body to store fat.

Ketogenic diet enables the body consume food that is satiating and filling

Those who have eaten ketogenic diet do find it extremely easy to limit calories. If you are using this diet in the right way, you will be able to consume quite a good amount of calories daily ranging from fats to protein which is both satiating and scrumptious. Those are in ketogenic diet would find it hard to consume enough food every day.

Finally, ketogenic diets have become more popular for many reasons. A part from helping weight loss, it is being considered as the possible treatment or prevention of epilepsy and researches have also shown that it can also be used in neurological conditions. Having known what the ketogenic diet is, you can try it if you have used it and you will be dumbfounded. Ketogenic diet is highly recommended.

Is the Ketogenic Diet Right For Me?

Benefits of the Ketogenic Diet

The benefits if ketogenic diet are numerous and happy ones. Some of the benefits one may expect after switching to ketogenic diet include:

It is always important to get a full blood lipid panel before starting on this diet so one can compare their blood work after starting on the diet.

Lower blood pressure

Ketogenic diets are effective in lowering the blood pressure. Though, if one is taking blood pressure medication, they should be aware that they begin to feel dizzy or tipsy from too much medication while on this diet. It is advisable for people suffering from blood pressure related diseases to seek a doctor's advice before starting on this diet

A drop in cholesterol

Cholesterol is usually made out of excess glucose. This diet requires one to consume less sugar foods which simply mean a reduction in the excess glucose. The body cholesterol will drop as the body has less glucose to make cholesterol

A drop in triglycerides

Consumption of carbohydrates is closely attached to triglycerides levels. This is the most well-known ketogenic diet advantage. The less the carbohydrates consumed, the lower the triglycerides readings will go. The triglycerides: HDL ratio is the best indicator of heart attack risk and is one of the blood test one should pay attention to. The best ration is 1:1 which suggests that one is healthy.

Weight loss

Adhering to a ketogenic diet plan might be extremely effective for normalizing your weight. However, if one has high fasting insulin, he/she may be required to add a high intensity program (an exercise one). Training has a high effect on increasing the sensitivity of the body to insulin.

What to watch out for on the diet

Disadvantages of ketogenic diet plan are mostly due to its side effects. Some of the side effects are extreme.

Frequent urination

This is because the body is burning the extra glycogen stored in the liver and muscles. This process releases a lot of water which is given out as urine.

Exhaustion and Dizziness

As the body gets rid of excess water, the body will lose minerals like salt, magnesium and potassium. Lower levels of these minerals will lead to a person becoming tired or very dizzy. This is amongst the well-known side effect of any low carbohydrate diet and the best way to overcome this is to keep replacing the minerals. This can be done by eating leafy vegetables (potassium), magnesium citrate (magnesium) or any other foods that contain the minerals.

Constipation

This is also common with most low carb diets and is usually caused by salt loss, dehydration and magnesium deficiency. This can be controlled by drinking more water and replacing the above minerals

Muscle cramps

This is due to loss of minerals particularly magnesium. It is therefore recommended that a person takes 3 slow discharge magnesium tablets like Slow-Mag for 20 days, and then keep on taking one tablet after wards

Diarrhea

There is need to limit the amount of fat you consume while on the ketogenic diet plan as this results to consuming more proteins. High proteins, low fat and low carbohydrate levels causes signs of "rabbit starvation". It is therefore advisable to replace the carbohydrates with fats, for example, butter or coconut oil and not proteins.

The Building Blocks of the Ketogenic Diet

A ketogenic diet is composed of a variety of foods that have their own health benefits and purposes. Many individuals with specific medical conditions or health goals prefer this diet because of its nutrition as well as having a variety of common foods that don't have to be eliminated from their original diet.

Proteins

A major part of the ketogenic diet is meat because it's the major source of protein. Beef, chicken and fish are important part of the diet because they supply the needed nutrients for the body. For individuals who aren't big fans of meat, tofu is also a great source of protein (and very common among vegans because it doesn't have any animal products). Cheese is also often eaten for its protein benefits but it also has some health set-backs like the high amount of calories and fat, so it's limited in the diet. Many other dairy products that are high in fat are eaten. Whole eggs are some of the most well-known contributors of protein in just about any diet. If possibly, try to purchase range-free eggs and you can also add them to other dishes.

Carbohydrates

Fruits and vegetables are the healthy and most common source of carbohydrates in this diet. Salads with leafy greens, green beans and carrots are the preferable vegetables. Peaches, berries and applause are the most common fruit that can be eaten alone by itself or added to other foods as a topping. Both vegetables and fruits also have many necessary vitamins and can be prepared many different ways, or even eaten uncooked. There are also many pasta substitutes that replace original whole grains, contributing with their nutrients. Spices like sea salt and black pepper also provide this important nutrient.

Fats

Fats compose the majority of the daily caloric intake in the ketogenic diet. They are very important to the body but some fats are very unhealthy and even dangerous to consume, so be cautious. To balance out the nutrients, foods like tuna and shellfish are commonly eaten. Some individuals also like to consume different types of oils (coconut, vegetable, olive, etc.) and add butters to their meat and other foods. Some of the healthiest sources of healthy fat are avocados, but you are also free to try almonds and other delicious nuts.

Beverages

In this diet, dehydration is fairly common so it's important to keep the body functioning properly with liquids. Of course the most basic liquid consumed by practically everyone is water, drink plenty of it! Sometimes coffee will provide a good energy boost as well. All types of teas are welcome, fruit, herbal or others. The more liquids in the body, the better. Liquid sweeteners like Stevia and Erythritol can be added to the tea or coffee for a sweet boost and extra flavor.

The Ketogenic diet is very unique and practically the opposite of the vegan diet. Make sure you consume all the nutrients you need for the day and this diet can have many positive effects on your health and body.

What to Avoid on the Ketogenic Diet

Many methods of losing some weight and maintaining a healthy and fitting body are evolving over time. Selecting the right diet, taking weight loss pills, doing exercises, and surgical methods are a few examples to get rid of excess fat cells from the body. While some of these methods may work perfectly, others may not only have insignificant effects, but also come with side-effects. One of the most effective methods is to practice the Ketogenic diet plan. It is a low-carbohydrate, adequate protein, and high-fat diet geared at burning excess fats. With this low carbohydrate diet plan, the aim is not to restrict intake of calories, but to reduce the amount of sugar and carbohydrate consumption.

What foods to avoid

On this plan, one should avoid food high in sugars, carbohydrates, and unhealthy fats. These diets are not only toxic to the human body, but they also supply the body with excess glucose that is then stored as fat cells. Since they raise blood sugars and insulin levels in the body, it becomes hard for the human body to lose more fats. In addition, human body digests and absorbs food high in carbohydrates faster than in fats or proteins. These processes not only lower metabolism, but also make the person hungry faster than normal, hence increasing the chances of the person consuming more calories that may lead to weight gain. The following is what to avoid on the ketogenic diet at all cost.

Junk or fast foods

These foods do not only contain high amounts of saturated salts and cholesterol, but they also lack essential nutrients the body require to remain healthy. Hot dogs, French fries, and soft sodas are a few examples of these foods. In addition, they contain chemicals and other substances that lower the body metabolism. With low metabolism, the body is unable to burn the food that a person takes, but instead stores it as fats. This effect does not only lead to weight gain, but to other complications such as hardening and narrowing of arteries hence resulting in high blood pressure or diabetes.

Some fruits and vegetables

One should avoid fruits that contain high amounts of carbohydrates. A few examples of such fruits are olive, watermelon, apricots, cranberry, bananas, and strawberry. It is also advisable to avoid the juices that come from these fruits since they do not only contain high carbohydrates, but they also have other artificial addictions harmful to the body. In addition, one should avoid vegetables that grow beneath the earth like onions, carrots, and potatoes for their high carbohydrate contents.

Alcohol

Even though the alcohol may contain no carbohydrates, research show that it slows down the fat burning processes in the body. It is better for one to take free sugar drinks like scotch and vodka, instead of alcohol.

Grain products

It is best for the person on the ketogenic diet to avoid grains and their products that contain high carbohydrates. Examples include white bread, white pasta, what rice, cakes, and pastries. In addition, avoid packaged or processed foods since they contain preservatives and other additions harmful to the body.

Frequently Asked Questions about the Ketogenic Diet

The ketogenic diet was founded in 1920 by Lyle McDonald. It is a very popular diet and is followed worldwide. The ketogenic diet is effective in preventing crises of many kinds as lesser carbohydrates from starches composed of glucose are consumed by the body. After this diet, it is necessary to avoid foods containing carbohydrates like bread, sugar, cereals, pasta and potatoes.

The ketogenic diet has been the staple food for people living in the countryside and also with the Eskimos and many tribes and who basically eat pure protein. During ketosis brain cells are able to get energy from fat instead of glucose. In fact the brain cannot consume fatty acids but uses only ketones or ketone bodies generated during fat metabolism.

Not only is the nervous system not damaged but it has been demonstrated by studies that brain ketosis acts as protective measure against toxic substances like free radicals and prevents hypoxia. Ketogenic diets are recommended by doctors to treat childhood epilepsy or diseases like Alzheimer.

The Ketogenic Diet

The ketogenic diet has been proven to work effectively for a third of patients who become tried and listless after very little effort. Controlled trials have established that a ketogenic diet is found to be effective in the treatment of severe epilepsy in children and adults. Although this diet is very popular among bodybuilders, it does not recommend consumption of foods which are rich in vitamins and minerals, such as broccoli, carrots, sweet potatoes, apples, grapes, raisins, figs, etc.

A Sample Meal Plan for the Ketogenic Diet

Breakfast - Two eggs, two slices of bacon and a boiled tomato.

Lunch - Hamburger meat wrapped in lettuce.

Dinner - Green beans, fried mushrooms and linseed oil with a salmon fillet red peppers.

Snacks - Unlimited yogurt and whole milk, cheese, strawberries with cream, peanut butter.

Frequently asked questions about the effects of a ketogenic diet:

Does the ketogenic diet have negative consequences in the liver or kidneys?

The ketogenic diet or diets based on eating fewer carbohydrates do not have any liver or renal type problems because it is a physiological process for which we are adapted by our own evolution and in fact people who have this type of problems are advised to take a ketogenic diet in many cases.

Is the ketogenic diet carcinogenic?

It has also been shown that the ketogenic diet helps shrink tumours and reduce the percentage of body fat and weight in the most obese people, yes factor that facilitates the development of cancer.

Does a ketogenic diet produce oxidation of cells?

Ketogenic diets increase the antioxidant capacity of the body is increased because oxygenate ketones mitochondria through activation of glutathione peroxidase producing an increase in the synthesis of mitochondrial glutathione. Antioxidants prevent the formation of free radicals thereby preventing oxidation and preventing cell death.

Is a ketogenic diet detrimental to participation in sports?

Many athletes use the ketogenic diet in combination with physical training and use key ketogenic supplements with their diet plan. This obviously needs some knowledge and experience and it is recommended to take the advice from a specialist in ketogenic diets and exercise.

The Ketogenic Diet and Diabetes

Before the invention of insulin in 1920s, the treatment of diabetes relied on dietary control. Diabetics were recommended to modify their diet to control the level of glucose in the blood circulation.

A ketogenic diet is comprised of low-carbohydrate amount. The diet has high fat content that supplements the carbohydrates. Fat is broken down and replaces glucose as a source of energy. The ketogenic diet has only enough protein for body growth.

Less carbohydrate in the diet lead the body to take measures and source for alternative source of energy. The liver releases stored glycogen that is converted to glucose. When the stores are exhausted the body turns to fatty acids replacing glucose.

Proteins are converted to glucose and the body is able to maintain normal blood sugar levels without ingesting carbohydrates. The body can effectively rely on fats for energy functions. Ingestion of insulin is accompanied by health problems. High insulin levels result to weight gain and fat storage sometimes accompanied by heart problems.

A ketogenic diet for diabetics is meant to reduce medical treatment of diabetes. Low carbohydrate in the diet prevents short term effects of diabetes and delays long term complications. The treatment of diabetes requires that medical attention is given continuously. Patients who manage their diet have a better chance of avoiding complications. Low carbohydrate diet leads to the benefit of weight loss and reduces the risk for cholesterol.

When carbohydrates are ingested, the body breaks them into glucose and other simple sugars. The glucose is taken into the blood system. A diet with more carbohydrates leads to toxic levels of blood sugar and the body responds by releasing insulin with the aim of converting glucose to glycogen for storage.

Diabetes occurs when the body does not produce enough insulin to cope with blood sugar after meals. The disease has become common of lately and the solution is to cut on carbohydrates and there will be no need for insulin.

Ketogenic diet is a complement of treatment for diabetes. This requirement of insulin can go as low as 50% easing the treatment procedure. The liver is able to produce glucose from proteins and the brain can rely on this. Some part of the brain only burns glucose for energy. Other parts of the body can rely entirely of fats for energy. With normal fat stores a person can go for days without eating.

Ketogenic diet appears to the body as starvation. The response is reduced insulin production. Oxidation of fatty acids increases to produce energy for body functions.

This method of diabetes treatment is advantageous because it deals with the root source. The aim is to reduce carbohydrates consumption, which is safer than injecting insulin to counteract high glucose level. The diet can be used where insulin is applied and faster results will be observed.

Fighting diabetes can be challenging because of the change in diet and lifestyle. The patients are sometimes mislead and filled with wrong information about the effect of ketogenic diet. It is hard to switch diet just because the doctor recommended. Managing the amount of carbohydrates and medication at the same time can maintain blood sugar for diabetics.

Putting It All Together

I hope you have found this guide to a ketogenic diet helpful and informative. With the proper diet and exercise regimen, you can see incredible changes in your body in very little time.

For any diet to work, you need to take action and stay committed. It is easy to have a cheat day here and there, especially when you are missing your favorite foods, but don't give in to the temptation. One cheat day often leads to another, and you find yourself suddenly not making any progress. Stick with it and believe in yourself. You can do it!

Preview of "Essential Oils" by Emily V. Steinhauser

Essential Oils

Essential oils are oils that are extracted from the flowers, leaves, fruits, peel, seeds, woods, bark, roots, and other natural materials. There are thousands of different kinds of essential oils, and each has unique properties and characteristics. They are highly volatile so they are easily absorbed by the skin. So one wants to take care in the use of them.

Many body care products contain essential oils that they use for their therapeutic properties, and not just for their scent. There are many essential oils that are an effective treatment for a number of different skin conditions. They are extremely concentrated and powerful. They can be regenerative both in physical and emotional ways, making you feel healthy and stronger. The benefits cannot be understated, essential oils can have a dramatic impact on how you look and feel.

This book will explore the various ways that one can use essential oils. I will also present the best oils to use in each specific situation, both from research and personal experience. Sections will focus on the using essential oils to treat, heal, and rejuvenate one's skin. We will also explore how to use essential oils to thicken one's hair, promote faster hair re-growth, and how to deal with hair loss.

Essential oils are often used therapeutically, and I will talk about the medicinal uses of essential oils. I will not only focus on physical application of the oils, but also on aromatherapy and the benefits it provides.

One of my favorite uses of essential oils is using them to deal with headaches, including migraines. They also prove efficacious for first aid, particularly in the reduction of swelling and the healing of bruises. I will also present information on how you can use essential oils to sharpen your mental focus, improve your concentration, and enhance your overall memory.

I am excited that you have joined me on this journey through the essential oils. I hope they bring you a long lifetime of improved health and comfort.

I hope you enjoyed the free preview of "Essential Oils" by Emily V. Steinhauser.

Preview of "Kindle Publishing Secrets Revealed" by James Chen

Learn to Make Money with Kindle Books

Passive income. We all want to make it. And publishing books on Amazon Kindle is a great way to do it. Imagine your books earning money 24 hours a day, 365 days a year on autopilot, leaving you the time to do whatever you desire. Sounds like a wonderful life, right?

It can be, and the first step is publishing your book. This book will guide you step by step through the process, from initial research to how to market your book.

Don't think you are a very good writer? I will show you how outsource your ideas to other writers who will write the books for you. All you need to do is publish them. And collect the checks.

I will also divulge a secret niche which sees extraordinary sales and searches on Amazon. There are very few writers taking advantage of this trick, and those who have are seeing their books in the bestseller lists. The best part: this niche only requires the books be between 15 to 30 pages in length. Short books, huge rewards.

Learn to take advantage of Amazon's enormous customer base, publishing books that will be searched for, found, and purchased. Learn to get your books to stand out from the millions of other ones already available in the Kindle store. It is simple: if people cannot find your books, they will not buy them. Learn how to be found.

The #1 Rule of Kindle Marketing

The rule is simple: find a process that makes money. And repeat it. Over and over again. This rule is particularly effective in terms of Kindle publishing. You publish your book, market it, let it make money, and do the entire process again.

Too many writers concentrate on one book. They invest all of their energy in making it perfect, trying to build up and audience, instead of writing additional books. Understand that having one book found within millions of books requires a whole lot of luck. But if you have two books, your odds increase. Think of each book as a lottery ticket, the more you have, the more likely you will have one hit the jackpot. Your goal should not be to have one book in the Kindle store, but hundreds. Don't imagine yourself as a writer, but as a publisher. And act accordingly.

Authors often focus on the visible success stories on Amazon, on the fiction writers who have sold hundreds of thousands of books. This is an incredibly small group, and their success is hard to replicate, because it was brought about by luck. You will most likely never get this lucky, so you need to create your own success. That means publishing a lot of books.

The people making money in the system are those who publish hundreds of books under different pen names. These books are often outsourced to a group of writers, as are the formatting and cover creation. This book encourages you to embrace the second method and act like a publisher, producing and selling as much content as you can.

Remember the more you publish, the larger your slice of the pie will be.

I hope you enjoyed the free preview of "Kindle Publishing Secrets Revealed" by James Chen.

Other Books Available From Gamma Mouse Media

Below you will find other popular Amazon bestsellers from Gamma Mouse Media.

Essential Oils – Emily V. Steinhauser

Forex Indicators – Warren R. Sullivan

Kindle Publishing Secrets Revealed – James Chen

Procrastination – Warren R. Sullivan

Brain Training Boot Camp – Warren R. Sullivan

Knee Pain Treatment – Emily V. Steinhauser

Marriage Problems – Emily V. Steinhauser

Quiet – Amelia Austin

Lust for Me – Amelia Austin

Cellulite Reduction – Emily V. Steinhauser

The Quick Start Guide to Macarons – Lindsay Stotts

Speed Reading Training – Warren R. Sullivan

Memory Enhancement – Warren R. Sullivan

The Quick Start Guide to Perfect Pancakes – Lindsay Stotts

Compulsive Hoarding – Emily V. Steinhauser

Printed in Great Britain
by Amazon.co.uk, Ltd.,
Marston Gate.